ISBN 978-0-243-31431-7
PIBN 10793243

1 MONTH OF
FREE
READING

at
www.ForgottenBooks.com

By purchasing this book you are eligible for one month membership to ForgottenBooks.com, giving you unlimited access to our entire collection of over 1,000,000 titles via our web site and mobile apps.

To claim your free month visit:
www.forgottenbooks.com/free793243

English
Français
Deutsche
Italiano
Español
Português

www.forgottenbooks.com

Mythology Photography **Fiction**
Fishing Christianity **Art** Cooking
Essays Buddhism Freemasonry
Medicine **Biology** Music **Ancient
Egypt** Evolution Carpentry Physics
Dance Geology **Mathematics** Fitness
Shakespeare **Folklore** Yoga Marketing
Confidence Immortality Biographies
Poetry **Psychology** Witchcraft
Electronics Chemistry History **Law**
Accounting **Philosophy** Anthropology
Alchemy Drama Quantum Mechanics
Atheism Sexual Health **Ancient History**
Entrepreneurship Languages Sport
Paleontology Needlework Islam
Metaphysics Investment Archaeology
Parenting Statistics Criminology
Motivational

PURPOSE OF THE SHRINE

1—To spread devotion to St. Jude Thaddeus, "Patron of Difficult Cases."

2—To educate worthy boys for the priesthood and foster love for the missions.

✠

SERVICES AT THE SHRINE

Every morning in the year a Mass is read for the Shrine intentions and those of the St. Jude Apostolate.

Every evening at 8 o'clock the Rosary and novena prayers are said by one of the Fathers;

Every Sunday afternoon at 3 o'clock a special Holy Hour in honor of St. Jude;

Every Thursday at 10:00 A.M. a Novena High Mass and at 12:00 noon a Novena Low Mass. Every Thursday at 6:30 and 8:00 P.M. Holy Hours and Novena Prayers.

✠

FIVE SOLEMN NOVENAS EACH YEAR
January, May, July, October, Lent

During these Novenas there are nine High Masses and nine Masses each day of the Novena, including a special Novena Mass at the Tomb of St. Jude Thaddeus in St. Peter's Basilica in Rome, Italy.

ST. JUDE THADDEUS

DEVOTIONAL EXERCISES

and

NOVENA PRAYERS

Revised Edition

Shrine of St. Jude Thaddeus
Conducted by the
DOMINICAN FATHERS
1909 South Ashland Avenue
Chicago 8, Illinois

ST. JUDE THADDEUS

THE FORGOTTEN SAINT, this is the title that is sometimes given to Saint Jude Thaddeus. It is hard to conceive how any saint of God could really be forgotten by men, yet it may be explained by a certain confusion of names. No doubt it was by reason of the shameful treason of another Jude, Judas Iscariot, that the name of a glorious apostle and martyr has suffered the forgetfulness of men. At all time, therefore, in this short sketch of our patron's life he will be called, not simply St. Jude, but St. Jude Thaddeus. Today more than ever is the power of St. Jude Thaddeus being revived in the minds and the hearts of men. He, in turn, is proving himself more than an ordinary advocate by, apparently, taking special delight in coming to the aid of persons in desperate need. Therefore, is he known as the "Patron in Desperate Cases." Although the name, St. Jude Thaddeus, has been neglected in the devotions of men it is nevertheless one of the oldest names in the calendar of the Church. It has the sanction of antiquity dating back to the call of the Apostles. It is found in the Canon of the Mass where he is called Thaddeus.

DEVOTION TO THE BLESSED VIRGIN MARY will be ever new and strong simply because she is the Mother of God. Nor will piety toward St. Joseph ever lessen, because he is the foster-father of Jesus Devotion to St. Jude Thaddeus, once it is known, should appeal to all for a similar reason: he also is closely associated with our Blessed Lord by blood relationship. This singular privilege came to him through Saints Joachim and Ann, the parents of the Blessed Virgin Mary. Being a grand-nephew of these two saints he is at once a nephew of Mary and Joseph which, of course, places him in the relationship of cousin to Our Lord Himself. Nearness to Christ is always a valuable and indispensable asset to a saint, but when it is the nearness of family relationship to the Savior of mankind, then is one sharply moved to endear himself to that saint.

ST. JUDE THADDEUS was the son of Cleophas and Mary of Cleophas. His mother brought him up in piety and innocence, both of which were fostered and increased by the example of Christ. This example was before him even in his boyhood days for, as cousin of the Savior he must have frequently associated with Him. What the life of St. Jude Thaddeus was up to the time of the call to the apostleship is not known, but this much is certain that when the divine invitation was extended to him he not only accepted it, but never for a moment did he allow his zeal as an apostle to cool. It was zeal and zeal alone

4

which eventually brought to him the much coveted reward of martyrdom. He was not only an apostle but also one of the sacred writers. His work is known as "The Epistle of St. Jude." Although only a very brief work of twenty-five verses, the shortest writing of the New Testament, "The Epistle of St. Jude," is remarkable for its strength and dignity. Most of its contents is well adapted to the present time, for the heresies and immoralities of those days are rampant today. It was against these things that St. Jude Thaddeus wrote. He closes his Epistle with admonitions for the Christians. It seems also that he was one of the last apostles to die. He implies this when he says: "Be mindful of the words which have been spoken before by the Apostles."

PROPER NAMES, in the early history of mankind, were used not only to designate a certain person but were often expressive of traits peculiar to that person. The several names ascribed to St. Jude Thaddeus explain the success that attended his apostolate. Saints Matthew and Mark call him Thaddeus. St. Luke in his Gospel and in the Acts of the Apostles calls him Jude, the brother of James, which name St. Jude Thaddeus calls himself in his Epistle. The name of Jude conveys the idea of praise and Thaddeus, according to St. Jerome, means a man of more than ordinary knowledge of the things of God. It also means sweetness and gentleness of character. A man endowed with these characteristics may truthfully call himself the "Servant of Jesus Christ." With praise of God on his lips and knowledge of Him in his heart, with gentleness of character, what an apostle he must have made!

ST. JUDE THADDEUS is generally shown with an image of Our Lord upon His breast. The tradition is that when the fame of Christ's miracles had reached the king of Edessa (in which country St. Jude Thaddeus preached and established the Church), the king who was afflicted with leprosy sent a messenger to Our Lord begging him to come and heal him. When the unfortunate king learned that he could not expect Christ to come to him he sent an artist to Jerusalem that he might at least get a portrait of the Master. On seeing Christ the poor artist was so blinded by the divine brightness of His face that he was unable to draw even a line. Jesus, moved with compassion and wishing to console the afflicted king, held a cloth to His face leaving thereon His own image. He then gave it to the poor artist telling him to carry it back to his ruler, at the same time promising to send some one to cure him. St. Jude Thaddeus was sent by Christ to perform the miracle. When St. Jude Thaddeus arrived he was immediately recognized. His first words of greeting to the king were: "Thou hast faith in the Lord Jesus; therefore, He sent me." St. Jude Thaddeus then laid his hand upon the king and the leprosy vanished immediately and completely. It is related that so great were the miracles St. Jude Thaddeus wrought that not only the king and his court, but well nigh the entire kingdom of Edessa were converted to the cause of Christ. This is the traditional explanation of the miniature of Christ on the breast of St. Jude Thaddeus. The details of St. Jude's life after the dispersal of the apostles from Jerusalem are matters solely of tradition and there is no intent to present them otherwise.

HIS LABORS IN PERSIA give some idea of the difficulties which were so often encountered in his ministry. This country was overrun with magicians who employed their arts to deceive the simple and foster pagan superstition. It was necessary that these imposters be exposed once and for all. St. Jude Thaddeus always found traces of two special agents of Satan who went before him trying to poison the minds of the people against him and therefore forestall the efficacy of his work. Their names were Zaroes and Arfaxat, skilled magicians, who by their trickery sought to dupe the ignorant into a belief in the power of pagan idols to hear and grant requests. The opportunity presented itself to make a complete exposure of the work of these magicians. God gave a special power to St. Jude Thaddeus. In his presence and at his command the idols were forced to speak and to confess the One True God. Then the demons inhabiting the idols were ordered to leave and in so doing the idols fell to the ground and

were broken into fragments amid a howl
of infernal rage. But it was the magicians
the Saint was anxious to meet face to face
that he might bring them to the justice of
God. On being informed that they were
in the camp of the Persian army, St. Jude
Thaddeus lost no time in gaining entrance
to the camp. Verardach, the commander-
in-chief, ordered St. Jude Thaddeus to ad-
vance and make known his mission. Fear-
less he cried out: "We serve Jesus Christ,
and have come to bring you eternal life
if you abandon your errors and your wor-
ship of the gods." It was a bold assertion
to make in the camp of an enemy, but the
commander was interested, owing to the
fact that he had already heard of the fall
of the pagan idols at the Saint's command.
The commander promised to hear more of
the mission of the Saint once the impend-
ing battle was over. Anxious to know the
outcome of the battle and thinking that
perhaps the Saint might enlighten him he
lost no time in approaching St. Jude
Thaddeus on the subject. The Saint com-
manded the idole to make reply to the
question. The answer came back that the
war would be long and tedious with great
losses on both sides. At this answer the
commander was very much disturbed.
Then the apostle with great joy exclaim-
ed: "Fear not, Oh Prince, thy gods lie!
Tomorrow at this very hour ambassadors
will arrive from the enemy's camp asking
terms of peace; they will accept all the
conditions you propose and will become

your subjects." So completely was his promise fulfilled that it was only the intercession of St. Jude Thaddeus that kept the two wicked magicians from being burned at the stake.

THROUGHOUT HIS ENTIRE MINISTRY St. Jude Thaddeus was subject to all sorts of persecution and suffering. Our Lord predicted this very thing concerning His apostles. Notwithstanding his great success it must be remembered that he at all times had to deal with a hard people, a people steeped in immorality. They were loath to surrender evil habits sanctioned by a custom of long standing. But the acceptance of Christianity meant new customs opposed to old customs, hence the doctrine of the All-pure Christ was offensive to their pagan ears. It was this very thing that was to bring about his martyr dom, and those unwilling to embrace the new doctrine waited impatiently for the day when vengeance could be meted out to him. The eventful day came, a day of victory for the enemies, but a day of great joy for St. Jude Thaddeus, now that the coveted prize was within reach. It is a custom in the Church to represent her martyrs in art with the instrument of torture that made possible their winning the crown of eternal glory. So we have St. Jude Thaddeus represented with a club in his hand, for it was with this weapon that he was put to death. Tradition tells that after death his head was severed from his body with a broadax. The church assures her children that his pure soul winged its way heavenward immediately after his martyrdom and that his name was written in letters of gold in the Book of Life.

HIS HOLY RELICS now lie in the great basilica of St. Peter in Rome. Pope Paul III, in a brief dated September 22, 1548, granted a plenary indulgence to all who would visit the tomb of St. Jude Thaddeus on his feast day, the day of his death, October 28. This is a very significant fact, for plenary indulgences were rarely granted at this period. It is a proof that his intercessory power with God must have been great. All the saints have power with God since they are the special friends of God. but the fact cannot be denied that some have been permitted to make their influence with God more visible than others. The reason for this rests with God alone. The history of St. Jude Thaddeus, both as to his life upon earth and his relation to his clients now, proves that God has vouchsafed him an extraordinary power in cases most desperate. It is especially in difficult cases that his wonderful help appears. Thousands have implored his aid and have received extraordinary answers to their prayers. Venerable Columba, a Dominican nun, was most devoted to St. Jude Thaddeus and she saw many a petition of grave and serious nature granted through his intercession. Another client among the saints was none other than the great St. Bernard. During his entire life he never ceased to invoke

St. Jude Thaddeus when trials and temptations surrounded him. When saint calls upon saint sinners should take courage and direction. Even though the difficulty be a malady defying all human skill, even though it be a sickness for which there is no apparent remedy, even though it be anguish of soul and distress of heart, poverty, misery or even despair, St. Jude Thaddeus, cousin of Jesus, will show a way out of the trouble, if it be according to the will of God. There is no problem so perplexing for which St. Jude Thaddeus, "Patron of Desperate Cases," cannot find a solution, thereby bringing joy and gladness to the heart.

MANY are the ways of gaining the favor of St. Jude Thaddeus. Some clients approach by making a weekly Holy Hour at the Shrine of St. Jude Thaddeus. Others make Novenas in his honor by assisting at Mass and receiving Holy Communion on nine consecutive days. Still others invoke him daily. It matters not the method used to obtain St. Jude Thaddeus' intercession just so one proves himself worthy of divine favor. St. Jude, pray for all who invoke thy aid! Help of the hopeless, aid them in their distress! Forgotten of Saints, forget not them who come to thee for help!

THE EPISTLE OF ST. JUDE

This Epistle was written between the years 62 and 67 A.D. as has been concluded from the text of the Epistle itself. It was occasioned by the teachings and practices of certain heretics within the Church and is a warning to them. After an Introduction (vv. 1-4), the first section (vv. 5-20) may be described as a Warning against False Teachers. The second section (vv. 21-25) is Admonitions for Christians. See C.C.D. edition of the New Testament, page 692.

✛

INTRODUCTION

1. Jude, the servant of Jesus Christ and the brother of James, to the called who have been loved in God the Father and preserved for Christ Jesus:
2. mercy and peace and charity be given you in abundance.
3. Beloved, while I was making every endeavor to write to you about our common salvation, I found it necessary to write to you, exhorting you to contend earnestly for the faith once
4. for all delivered to the saints. For certain men have stealthily entered in, who long ago were marked out for this condemnation, ungodly men who turn the grace of God into wantonness and disown our only Master and Lord, Jesus Christ.

WARNING AGAINST FALSE TEACHERS

5. But I desire to remind you, though once for all you have come to know all things, that Jesus, who saved the people from the land of Egypt, the next time destroyed those who did
6. not believe. And the angels also who did not preserve their original state, but forsook their abode, he has kept in everlasting chains under darkness for the judgment of the great day.
7. Just as Sodom and Gomorrah, and the neighboring cities which like them committed sins of immorality and practised unnatural vice, have been made an example, undergoing the punishment of eternal fire.
8. In like manner do these men also defile the flesh, disregard authority, de-
9. ride majesty. Yet when Michael the archangel was fiercely disputing with the devil about the body of Moses, he did not venture to bring against him an accusation of blasphemy, but said,
10. "May the Lord rebuke thee." But these men deride whatever they do not know; and the things they know by instinct like the dumb beasts, become for them a source of destruction.
11. Woe to them! for they have gone in the way of Cain, and have rushed on thoughtlessly into the error of Balaam for the sake of gain, and have perished in the rebellion of Core.

12. These men are stains on their feasts. banqueting together without fear, looking after themselves; clouds without water, carried about by the winds; trees in the fall, unfruitful,

13. twice dead, uprooted; wild waves of the sea, foaming up their shame; wandering stars, for whom the storm of darkness has been reserved forever.

14. Now of these also Henoch, the seventh from Adam, prophesied, saying, "Behold the Lord has come with

15. thousands of his holy ones to execute judgment upon all, and to convict all the impious of all their impious works, and of all the hard things that impious sinners have spoken against

16. him." These are grumbling murmurers walking according to their lusts. And haughty in speech, they culti-

17. vate people for the sake of gain. But as for you, beloved, be mindful of the words that have been spoken beforehand by the apostles of our Lord

18. Jesus Christ, who kept saying to you that at the end of time there will come scoffers, walking impiously

19. according to their desires. These are they who set themselves apart, sensual men, not having the Spirit.

ADMONITIONS FOR CHRISTIANS

20. But as for you, Beloved, build up yourselves upon your most holy faith,

21. praying in the Holy Spirit. **Keep**

yourselves in the love of God, looking for the mercy of our Lord Jesus
22. Christ unto life everlasting. And
some, who are judged, reprove;
23. but others, save, snatching them from
the fire. And to others be merciful
with fear, hating even the garment
which is soiled by the flesh.

CONCLUSION

24. Now to Him who is able to preserve
you without sin and to set before the
presence of his glory, without blem-
25. ish, in gladness, to the only God our
Savior, through Jesus Christ our
Lord, belong glory and majesty
dominion and authority, before all
time, and now, and forever. Amen.

DEVOTIONAL PRAYERS
TO ST. JUDE THADDEUS
NOVENA PRAYERS
FOR SERVICES AT THE SHRINE

Recitation of The Rosary

In the Name of the Father, and of the Son, and of the Holy Ghost. Amen.

O glorious apostle, St. Jude Thaddeus, true relative of Jesus and Mary, I salute thee through the most Sacred Heart of Jesus! Through this Heart I praise and thank God for all the graces He has bestowed upon thee. Humbly prostrate before thee, I implore thee through this Heart to look down upon me with compassion. Oh, despise not my poor prayer; let not my trust be confounded! To thee God has granted the privilege of aiding mankind in the most desperate cases. Oh, come to my aid, that I may praise the mercies of God! All my life I will be grateful to thee and will be thy faithful client until I can thank thee in heaven. Amen.

Priest: "Blessed Apostle, with confidence we invoke thee!"

People: "Blessed Apostle, with confidence we invoke thee!"

Priest: "St. Jude, help of the hopeless, aid us in our distress!"

People: "St. Jude, help of the hopeless, aid us in our distress!"

Pray for us, that before death we may expiate all our sins by sincere repentance and the worthy reception of the holy sacraments!

Pray for us, that we may appease the Divine Justice and obtain a favorable judgment!

Pray for us, that we may be admitted into the company of the blessed to rejoice in the presence of our God forever!

Most holy apostle, St. Jude Thaddeus, faithful servant and friend of Jesus, the name of the traitor who delivered thy beloved Master into the hands of His enemies has caused thee to be forgotten by many, but the Church honors and invokes thee universally as the patron of hopeless cases and of things despaired of. Pray for me who am so miserable; make use, I implore thee, of that particular privilege accorded to thee to bring visible and speedy help where help is almost despaired of. Come to my assistance in this great need that I may receive the consolations and succor of heaven in all my necessities, tribulations and sufferings, particularly (here make your request) and that I may bless God with thee and all the elect throughout eternity.

I promise thee, O blessed Jude, to be ever mindful of this great favor, and I will never cease to honor thee as my special and powerful patron and to do all in my power to encourage devotion to thee **Amen.**

*Our Father, Hail Mary, Glory be to the Father,
etc., three times.*

Priest: St. Jude Thaddeus, pray for us!
People: And for all who invoke thy aid!

PRAYER FOR A HAPPY DEATH

O, my Lord and Savior, support me
in that hour in the strong arms of Thy
Sacraments, and by the Fresh fragrance
of Thy consolations. Let the absolving
words be said over me, and the holy oil
sign and seal me, and Thy own Body be
my food, and Thy Blood my sprinkling;
and let my sweet Mother, Mary, breathe
on me, and my Angel whisper peace to me,
and my glorious Saints -smile on me;
that in them all and through them all,
I may receive the gift of perseverance, and
die, as I desire to live, in Thy faith, in Thy
Church, in Thy service, and in Thy love.
Amen.—*Cardinal Newman.*

May he support us all the day long, till
the shades lengthen, and the evening
comes, and the busy world is hushed, and
the fever of life is over, and our work is
done! Then in His mercy may He give
us a safe lodging, and a holy rest, and
peace at the last!—*Cardinal Newman.*

NOVENA PRAYERS
FOR PRIVATE DEVOTIONS
LITANY OF ST. JUDE THADDEUS

Lord, have mercy on us!
Christ, have mercy on us!
Lord, have mercy on us!

Christ, hear us!
Christ, graciously hear us!
God, the Father of heaven, have mercy on us!
God, the Son, Redeemer of the world, have mercy on us!
God, the Holy Ghost, have mercy on us!
Holy Trinity, one God. have mercy on us!
St. Jude, relative of Jesus and Mary, pray for us!
St. Jude, while on earth deemed worthy to see Jesus and Mary and to enjoy their company, pray for us!
St. Jude, raised to the dignity of an apostle, pray for us!
St. Jude, who hadst the honor of beholding thy Divine Master humble Himself to wash thy feet, pray for us!
St. Jude, who at the Last Supper didst receive Holy Communion from the hands of Jesus, pray for us!
St. Jude, who after the profound grief which the death of thy beloved Master caused thee, hadst the consolation of beholding Him risen from the dead, and of assisting at His glorious Ascension, pray for us!
St. Jude, who wast filled with the Holy Ghost on the day of Pentecost, pray for us!
St. Jude, who didst preach the Gospel in Persia, pray for us!
St. Jude, who didst convert many people to the Faith, pray for us!
St. Jude, who didst perform wonderful

miracles in the power of the Holy Spirit, pray for us!

St. Jude, who didst restore an idolatrous king to health, both of soul and body, pray for us!

St. Jude, who didst impose silence on demons, and confound their oracles, pray for us!

St. Jude, who didst foretell to a weak prince an honorable peace with his powerful enemy, pray for us!

St. Jude, who didst take from deadly serpents the power of injuring man, pray for us!

St. Jude, who disregarding the threats of the impious, didst courageously preach the doctrine of Christ, pray for us!

St. Jude, who didst gloriously suffer martyrdom for the love of thy Divine Master, pray for us!

Blessed apostle, with confidence, we invoke thee!

Blessed apostle, with confidence, we invoke thee!

Blessed apostle, with confidence, we invoke thee!

St. Jude, help of the hopeless, aid us in our distress!

St. Jude, help of the hopeless, aid us in our distress!

St. Jude, help of the hopeless, aid us in our distress!

That by thy intercession both priests and people of the Church may obtain an ardent zeal for the Faith of Jesus Christ, we beseech thee, hear us!

That thou wouldst defend our **Sovereign** Pontiff and obtain peace and unity for the Holy Church, we beseech thee, hear us!

That all heathens and unbelievers may be converted to the true Faith, we beseech thee, hear us!

That faith, hope and charity may increase in our hearts, we beseech thee, hear us!

That we may be delivered from all evil thoughts, and from all the snares of the devil, we beseech thee, hear us!

That thou wouldst vouchsafe to aid and protect all those who honor thee, we beseech thee hear us!

That thou wouldst preserve us from all sin and from all occasion of sin, we beseech thee, hear us!

That thou wouldst defend us at the hour of death, against the fury of the devil and his evil spirits, we beseech thee, hear us!

Lamb of God, Who takest away the sins of the world, spare us, O Lord.

Lamb of God, Who takest away the sins of the world, graciously hear us, O Lord.

Lamb of God, Who takest away the sins of the world, have mercy on us.

Pray for us, Blessed Jude,

That we may be made worthy of **the** promises of Christ.

LET US PRAY

O St. Jude Thaddeus, thou **relative of** Jesus Christ, thou **glorious apostle and**

martyr, renowned for thy virtues and
miracles, faithful and prompt intercessor
of all who honor thee and trust in thee!
Thou art a powerful patron and helper in
grievous afflictions. I come to thee and
entreat thee from the depths of my heart;
come to my aid with thy powerful intercession, for thou hast received from God
the privilege to assist with thy manifest
help, those who almost despair of all hope.
Look down upon me; my life is a life of
crosses, my days are days of tribulation,
and my heart is an ocean of bitterness. All
my paths are strewn with thorns and
scarcely one moment passes but is witness
of my tears and sighs; uneasiness, discouragement, mistrust, and almost despair
prey upon my soul.

Thou canst not forsake me in this sad
plight. I will not depart from thee until
thou hast heard me. Oh! hasten to my aid.
I will be grateful to thee all my life. I
will honor thee as my special patron, I
will thank God for the graces bestowed
upon thee, and will encourage devotion to
thee according to my power. Amen.

St. Jude Thaddeus, pray for us.
And for all who invoke thy aid.

✝

PRAYER OF THANKSGIVING
(To Be Said When a Favor has Been Granted)

O most sweet Lord Jesus Christ, in
union with the unutterable heavenly

22

praise with which the Most Holy Trinity extols itself and which thence flows upon Thy Sacred Humanity, upon Mary, upon all the angels and saints, I praise, glorify and bless Thee for all the graces and privileges Thou has bestowed upon Thy chosen apostle and intimate friend, St. Jude Thaddeus. I pray Thee, for the sake of his merits, grant me Thy grace, and through his intercession come to my aid in all my needs, but especially at the hour of my death deign to strengthen me against the rage of my enemies. Amen.

Our Father, Hail Mary, Glory be to the Father, etc., three times.

✝

PRAYER TO
ST. JUDE THADDEUS

O Glorious St. Jude Thaddeus, by those sublime privileges, which so ennobled thee in thy lifetime—relationship according to the flesh with Our Lord Jesus Christ, and the apostolate; by that glory which, as the reward of thy labours and martyrdom, thou dost now enjoy in heaven, obtain for us from the Giver of all good things the favours spiritual and temporal of which we have need, to enable us to acquire the treasure of that divinely inspired doctrine, which thou hast set before us in thy Epistle, and so, to build the edifice of perfection upon the foundation of the Faith, by prayer and the help of the

Holy Spirit. Enable us to keep ourselves always in the love of God, looking for the mercy of Jesus Christ unto life everlasting, and to help by every available means those who stray from the truth. Thus shall we exalt the glory, the majesty, the empire, the might of Him, who can preserve us without sin, and keep us without blemish and in gladness for the coming of Our Lord Jesus Christ, Our Divine Savior. Amen.

(300 *days, once a day—Preces et Pia Opera,* 1938.)

✠

HOW TO MAKE A NOVENA

Solemn Novena of (9) Consecutive Days

Attend one of the exercises at the Shrine for the nine days. As there are several exercises a day choose the hour designated on the leaflet most convenient for you, but you need not attend the same service each day should another service at the Shrine be more suitable on that particular day. Follow the exercises as they are conducted. You should, if at all possible, go to confession and communion during the novena. If you can't go to communion at the regular Novena Mass you may receive in your own church. Should unforeseen circumstances make it impossible to attend one of the novena services, the novena prayers should be said at home on that one day. Those out of town can and should say the novena prayers at home during the nine days.

PRIVATE NOVENA DURING THE YEAR OUTSIDE OF SOLEMN NOVENA TIME

Everything stated above applies except that the prayers are recited privately at home, in church or if possible at the Shrine.

✛

NOVENA OF NINE THURSDAYS OR SUNDAYS

Start your novena on one particular Thursday or Sunday and persevere for nine consecutive Thursdays or Sundays. For those living in Chicago, novena services are conducted by the Dominican Fathers for the convenience of people, every Thursday, at 10:00 A. M., 12:00 Noon, 6:30 and 8:00 P.M., and every Sunday afternoon at three. You may start a private novena on any day. Mass is celebrated every morning at the Shrine by one of the Fathers for such intentions.

Should you desire Special Masses in honor of St. Jude in Novena form for your personal intentions, the following is to be observed: Stipend for nine low Masses should be mailed into the Dominican Fathers. High Masses also can be arranged for. Specific dates will be given for the latter, but not for the former. The same holds for a triduum of Masses (3 consecutive Masses.)

For any of the above Novenas votive lights can be arranged for so that they burn at the Shrine during your novena.

HYMN TO ST. JUDE

(Sung to the Melody of "Dear Guardian of Mary"
—St. Basil's Hymnal)

Apostle of Jesus,
A martyr saint of old,
The cousin of Our Savior,
Of Whom thy love hath told;
A writer of the scriptures
With tongues of fire aflame.
‖The worker great of wonders‖
‖In Jesus Holy Name.‖

St. Jude, though oft forgotten
Thou shalt remembered be;
We hail thee now in glory
And have recourse to thee
For help for the despairing
When hopeless seems the task.
‖And from the Heart of Jesus‖
‖Through thee we favors ask.‖

BENEDICTION HYMNS

O SALUTARIS

O Salutaris Hostia,
  Quae coeli pandis ostium:
Bella premunt hostilia,
  Da robur, fer auxilium.
Uni trinoque Domino
  Sit sempiterna gloria:
Qui vitam sine termino
  Nobis donet in patria. Amen.

✠

TANTUM ERGO

Tantum ergo Sacramentum
  Veneremur cernui;
Et antiquum documentum
  Novo cedat ritui;
Praestet fides supplementum
  Sensuum defectui.

Genitori, Genitoque,
  Laus et jubilatio.
Salus, honor, virtus quoque
  Sit et benedictio;
Procedenti ab utroque
  Compar sit laudatio. Amen.

V. Panem de coelo praestitisti eis.
                            (Alleluia.)

R. Omne delectamentum in se habentem.
                            (Alleluia.)

At end of prayer—Amen

HYMN
HOLY GOD WE PRAISE THY NAME!

Holy God, we praise Thy Name,
Lord of all, we bow before Thee.
All on earth Thy sceptre claim,
All in heaven above adore Thee,
‖Infinite Thy vast domain,‖
‖Everlasting is Thy reign.‖

Hark, the loud celestial hymn
Angel choirs above are raising;
Cherubim and Seraphim,
In unceasing chorus praising,
‖Fill the heavens with sweet accord,‖
‖Holy. Holy, Holy Lord.‖

PRAYER FOR A HOLY LIFE BY
ST. THOMAS AQUINAS

Grant me, O merciful God, that what is pleasing to Thee I may ardently desire, prudently examine, truthfully acknowledge, and perfectly accomplish for the praise and glory of Thy name. Ordain, O my God, my whole life, and what Thou requirest that I should do, grant me to know it and to fulfil it as is meet and profitable to my soul. Give me Thy grace, O Lord my God, that I may not fail in prosperity or in adversity, avoiding pride in the former and discouragement in the latter. May I rejoice in nothing but what leads to Thee, grieve for nothing what turns away from Thee. May I wish to please and fear to displease none but Thee.

May I despise, O Lord, all transitory things, and prize only that which is eternal. May I shun any joy that is without Thee, nor wish for anything outside of Thee. May I delight in no rest which is without Thee. Grant me, O my God, to direct my heart toward Thee, and in my failings constantly grieve, with the purpose of amendment.

Make me, O Lord, my God, obedient without contradiction, poor without depression, chaste without corruption, patient without murmuring, humble without pretence, cheerful without dissipation, mature without dullness, prompt without levity, fearing Thee without despair, truthful without duplicity, doing good without presumption, correcting my neighbor without haughtiness, and edifying him by word and example without hypocrisy.

Give me, O Lord God, a watchful heart, which no curious thought will turn away from Thee; a noble heart, which no unworthy affection will drag down; a righteous heart, which no irregular intention will twist aside; a firm heart, which no tribulation will break; a free heart, which no violent affection will claim for itself.

Grant me, finally, O Lord my God, science in knowing Thee, diligence in seeking Thee, wisdom in finding Thee, a conduct pleasing to Thee, a perseverance trustfully awaiting Thee, and a confidence finally embracing Thee. May I endure Thy punishments by penitence; profit by Thy benefits by grace in this world, and enjoy Thy blessedness by glory in the next; Who livest and reignest, true God, forever and ever. Amen.

PRAYER FOR
THE SICK AND THE DYING

O Most merciful Jesus, Lover of Souls, I pray Thee by the agony of Thy most Sacred Heart and by the sorrows of Thy Immaculate Mother, cleanse in Thy Blood the sinners of the whole world who are now in their agony and are to die this night. "Heart of Jesus, once in agony, have mercy on the sick and the dying." (100 days, Pius IX.)

✝

BLESSING FOR THE SICK

Grant almighty and eternal God, everlasting health to those who believe. Hear us for Thy sick, for whom we implore the aid of Thy tender mercy, that being restored to bodily health they may give thanks to Thee in Thy church, through Christ our Lord. Amen.

They shall lay their hands upon the sick and they shall recover, may Jesus, the son of Mary, the Lord and Redeemer of the world, through the merits and intercession of His Holy apostle Jude and all His saints show them favor and mercy. Amen.

31

PRAYER BEFORE A CRUCIFIX

Look down upon me, good and gentle Jesus, while before Thy face I humbly kneel, and with burning soul pray and beseech Thee to fix deep in my heart lively sentiments of faith, hope, and charity, true contrition for my sins and a firm purpose of amendment; and while I contemplate with great love and tender pity Thy five wounds, pondering over them within me and calling to mind the words which David, Thy prophet, said of Thee, my Jesus: "They have pierced My hands and My feet; they have numbered all my bones."

(Plenary Indulgence, applicable to the souls in Purgatory, if said before a crucifix. after Holy Communion.)

The Apostolate

1. You may send your petition **ANY TIME** with the request that it be placed on the Shrine Altar near the Sacred Relic, and prayed for during your own novenas made publicly or privately at home. YOU are urged to make us aware of your thanksgiving.

2. If you desire a novena of **VOTIVE LIGHTS** to be burned before the Shrine, during your own novenas, — $1.00 will cover the expense.

3. By joining the St. Jude Apostolate whose yearly members contribute $1.00 per year toward the education of worthy candidates for the priesthood you enjoy every spiritual benefit of the Shrine as well as all the good works, Masses, prayers of the Dominican Fathers and Novices and Students of the Province of St. Albert the Great.

4. Those who make an offering of $10.00 are considered perpetual benefactors of the Dominican Order, and PERPETUAL MEMBERS of the APOSTOLATE.

5. The Dominican Fathers will be pleased to receive Gregorian Masses at any time to be offered for the dead.

SHRINE of
ST. JUDE THADDEUS

"Patron of Difficult Cases"

DOMINICAN FATHERS
1909 So. Ashland Ave.
Chicago, 8, Illinois

St. Jude Thaddeus : devotional exercises and novena prayers

Dominicans

C1532024

Boston College Libraries

[6] stjudethaddeusd

May 08, 2014

CPSIA information can be obtained
at www.ICGtesting.com
Printed in the USA
LVHW030726210219
608162LV00017B/1283/P